E.P.N.

Ewen Prime Network

~

Sell Your Book !

By

David K. Ewen, M.Ed.

Magazine
Online Radio
Web Television

Samples

The internet continues to grow and provide fantastic content to help authors and publishers sell books.   At EPN, the internet is the platform that provides a magazine, three radio shows. Beginning in 2010, we are taking author success to the next level.

TAN Magazine

> http://todaysauthor.livejournal.com

Radio Shows

> http://www.blogtalkradio.com/ewenprime

> *In 2008, I launched & hosted five radio shows on COS*

> http://www.blogtalkradio.com/Circle-Of-Seven

TV on Web

Here are some earlier versions of TV on web before EPN

> **http://www.youtube.com/watch?v=LILKzQLApus**

> **http://www.youtube.com/watch?v=l5-Mrt82hGw**

Do a video search for Today's Author with David Ewen.   You will see a lot.

Ewen Prime Network

Sell Your Book !

By   David K. Ewen, M.Ed.

David K. Ewen, M.Ed.

I launched my publishing company in 1994 by gathering writers, editors, and illustrators to produce poetry and books for children. The first book produced was "Diving Into Music Without Actually Drowning". In 1998, the book "The Doll House" resulted in the author becoming an award winner in the Boston area. Many others books have served as a voyage of great experience in publishing.

In 1998, I found ways to support self-published authors and the independent publishing industry by founding The New England Publishers Association. Part of my role was to conduct a year long speaking tour in all six New England states to support authors and their efforts to reach out to their reading audience.

At the studios of WORC 1310 AM & WGFP 940 AM my talk show "Author of The Week" began my journey as a talk show host supporting authors that continues to this very day. My book "Become A Talk Show Host" demonstrates my passion

In 2004, writers started to become authors in my college class "Publish Your Book - Guaranteed". I've been at eleven universities and colleges in four states. My book, "Let's Make It Simple", is now in it's third edition.. Both the class and book have been successful even during the toughest economic times since the Great Depression.

Now my latest venture EPN supports the success of authors and publishing industry experts to reach their audience. I'm excited to pull my experience together and work toward your success. I get a rush from hearing success stories from people I've helped in the publishing world.

Purpose of Book

For well over a decade I've worked in the media to promote authors and publishing industry experts. Being a talk show host is one of my many passions. Before every show, I've had a pre-show conference call or one-on-one support session to break the ice and ensure the light shines effectively for my guests.

How Will Your Book End Up?

How will your book end up? There is not one single answer to that. Every author is different as to how he/she see themselves and where they expect the success of their book to be in the future. The final reality is dependent on how the audience is properly identified and how to reach them is best understood. In addition, it is necessary to understand the basic mechanics of book publishing and the independent press industry. Also, it is important to understand that the business of publishing is a balance between cost verses risk. This is true in any business.

Reality

Writers believe their writing is a work of art. It is! To reach a market requires marketing techniques much greater than saying, "It's great!"   Consumers always, always, always ask "What's in it for me?" ** "WIFFM" RULE **   If you can't answer that question to a diverse population, then your statement "It's great!" is assumed false.

Let's understand the realistic outcome of published works. According to one of Publisher Weekly's survey of five large publishers, only one in ten of their fiction books make a profit. The 10% that do succeed pays for the success of the failure of the remaining 90%. Even in mid-sized publishers, as many as 60% of all general trade titles may lose money.   As David R. Godine admits, only 40% of the sixty titles he publishes each year are likely to be profitable.

Your potential readers ask the question, **"What's in it for me?"**. That's called **W.I.I.F.M.** in business. It's the same question you ask when considering a purchase. You should expect your readers to do the same.   It's reality.

WIIFM = **What's In It For Me** ?   Do you have the answer? If you can answer it in the format below, you'll reach your audience.

WIIFM   =   (It/This) will (Make/Give) you ___result or emotion__

WIIFM = What's In It For Me ?

Below are some examples of WIIFM. Those examples are simple, but you can out perform the example to make your book a greater success for your readers. Take a look below.

- It will make you at peace
- This will give you success
- It will make you inspired
- This will make you happy

Why not give it a try. It's not as easy as you think. That's right, it's not easy. I know because I've been teaching it to my students who at first thought it was easy since 2004. Make efforts to brainstorm and come up with five WIIFM's for your readers. Then do it again so that you are finally happy with the results. Yes, that's right, do it again and get it right to your satisfaction and your potential reader's satisfaction. Can you give it a try?

WIIFM = (It/This) will (Make/Give) you ___result or emotion__

Can you explain why reader's should care about your book? Do you know how to explain what your book gives readers?

What Is E.P.N. ?

EPN is E*wen* P*rime* N*etwork*.   It is a content provider that includes   publishing company, a magazine, three online radio shows (so far), and web TV programs.

Since 1998, I've been in the media as a talk show host.   I remember "Author of The Week" on both radio and TV.   For well over ten years, I've held interviews with New York Times best selling authors, publishing industry experts, major newspapers, a man that walked on the moon, and another astronaut that helped build the international space station.   I've talked with giants like former Secretary of Defense Casper Weinberger.

I have come to learn that authors always have an interesting story to tell that explains their contribution to the written word and books for readers.   I like to carry that in an interview and have a listening audience get the thrill of talking with someone who demonstrates a passion for their work.

From years of promoting authors in the media, I have developed a style that has been appreciated and respected.   Now it's time to take the skill to the next level that is long over due.

Because EPN uses three different types of media available on the internet, authors can more effectively reach their reading audience. The book selling tool for authors has been the interview, be it the feature article in the news paper, a talk on radio, or being featured on Oprah.   That is where my talent comes in.   I've been a talk show host since 1998 and have a passion to make authors more effective in getting their books out.   I do the same for experts in the publishing industry.

Elements of E.P.N.

Let's see what EPN is all about.   The simple outline below will show all that you will be involved with to promote your book or expertise in the publishing industry.

Publishing Company

> Ewen Prime Company (est 1994)

Magazine

> TAN Magazine (Today's Author News)

Three Online Radio Shows

> Today's Author - Profile author and book
> Night View - Focus on author's passion for topic
> Morning Coffee - call in show to talk with author

Web TV program

> Author Of The Week - Video of author, book & talk

Imagine doing all that without having to travel.   All interviews that help sell your book involves first understanding the process, then doing all the work from home.

What You Get

The audience can

1. Read about you and your book in ***TAN Magazine***
2. Discover your book on ***Today's Author (radio)***
3. Get acquainted with you on ***Night View (radio)***
4. Speak with you on ***Morning Coffee (radio)***
5. Watch you and your book (web TV)

Your Participation In Marketing

Since the dawn of publishing it has always been the publisher or publishing industry expert who had to speak their voice to sell product or service.   Today the technology is different, however the philosophy remains unchanged.   Now with the internet, the vision to sell more has changed.   Print-on-demand and other digital technologies has placed authors in a larger ocean of content for readers to choose from.   If the internet is used more effectively as social media sites intent, then authors can reach those readers.   That's where EPN comes in.

EPN combines the tools of the internet and the media to make an effective marketing campaign.   I've been working on it since 1998.   I've learned to make you successful, I can't do it alone. Using my tools and informative resources from you, your book or industry expertise will have a powerful voice.   It's another way of saying the old cliché said in so many ways: *"Don't work harder. Think smarter"*

At eleven universities and colleges in four states, I've taught writers and authors how to sell books since 2004.   Today, I'm using all the media tools that I've worked with since 1998 to make you effective.   I really want you to succeed.   I'll show you how your knowledge partnered with EPN will make positive results happen.   Allow yourself the confidence to make you succeed.

<u>Your First Steps</u>

To support you, information and material can only come from you. I've outlined what is needed below.   This is the first set of tools to help you make

Pictures sent in JPEG format.

* Face picture of author
* Above waist of author holding book
* Face picture of author holding book
* Cover of book

Explain in one short sentence why readers should get your book.

Explain in another single short sentence why readers should get your book.

Where is your book available online?   Amazon?   Your web site?   Ebay?   Online at Barnes and Noble or Borders?   Other site?

<u>Selling The Author</u>

- **RASCIL**
- **WIIFM**
- **5 W's**

RASCIL

Reliability, Authenticity, Simplicity, Completeness, Location

WIIFM

What's In It For Me

(It/This) will (Make/Give) you __results/emotion__

5 W's

Who, What, When, Where, Why

<u>RASCIL</u>

R = Reliability

How long have you been an expert?

A = Authenticity

Certifications or other credible evidence

S = Simplicity

How easy is it to get the book.   What about the book is simple

C = Completeness

What are all the benefits from the features of the book

I = Illustration

Good cover for good packaging

L = Location

Where can the book be found (online, store, etc)

Practice: RASCIL

R = Reliability

_____

A = Authenticity

_____

S = Simplicity

_____

C = Completeness

_____

I = Illustration

_____

L = Location

_____

Think Of Another Way to Use RASCIL

R = Reliability

How long have you been an expert?

A = Authenticity

Certifications or other credible evidence

S = Simplicity

How easy is it to get the book. What about the book is simple

C = Completeness

What are all the benefits from the features of the book

I = Illustration

Good cover for good packaging

L = Location

Where can the book be found (online, store, etc)

More Practice: RASCIL

R = Reliability

_____

A = Authenticity

_____

S = Simplicity

_____

C = Completeness

_____

I = Illustration

_____

L = Location

_____

WIIFM = What's In It For Me (The Reader)

WIIFM = (It / This) will (Make / Give) You ___ result / Emotion

Remember the examples mentioned earlier?

- It will make you at peace
- This will give you success
- It will make you inspired
- This will make you happy

Create some examples for your book

It will Make you _____

This will give you _____

It will give you _____

This will make you _____

WIIFM = What's In It For Me (The Reader)

WIIFM = (It / This) will (Make / Give) You ___ result / Emotion

It's easy to explain how to use WIIFM, but I fully understand it's to put into normal practice.

Let's do some more

It will Make you _____

This will give you _____

It will give you _____

This will make you _____

WIIFM = What's In It For Me (The Reader)

WIIFM = (It / This) will (Make / Give) You ___ result / Emotion

Try it again !

<u>Let's do some more</u>

        It will Make you _____

        This will give you _____

        It will give you _____

        This will make you _____

<u>5 W's - You can call it "Journalism 101"</u>

The 5 W's is what I call Journalism 101.   It is the most basic reporting style, but provides a complete story about you and your book.   It's good to be in the practice of speaking the language of the media when working with magazines, radio, and TV, including EPN.

The 5 W's are:

- Who?
- What?
- When?
- Where?
- Why?

You may also want to consider adding and "H" for **How**

<u>5 W's</u>   =   Who, What, When, Where, Why

WHO: Your Name
                Your Title
                Who you are

WHAT: **What Happened**

                Your Book Title
                Your Special Project
                RASCIL Factors (See next page)

WHEN: **When A Situation Can or Did Happen**

                When Your Book Will Be Published
                How Long You Have Been …

WHERE: A Location For A Cause or Event

                Where You Are From

WHY: **The passion (WIIFM) "What's In It For Me" (for the reader)**

                WIIFM = (It/This) will (Give/Make) you __results/emotion__

Practice: Putting It All Together

Using RASCIL factors, you can provide the "Who" and the "What".   Using WIIFM, you can provide the "Why".   The When and Where is simply a time frame and location.

RASCIL >>>   WHO

RASCIL >>>   WHAT

WHEN

WHERE

WHY   <<< WIIFM

We will practice putting together RASCIL, 5 W's and WIIFM.

Practice: Putting It All Together

RASCIL >>>	**WHO**
RASCIL >>>	**WHAT**
	WHEN
	WHERE
	WHY <<< WIIFM

RASCIL = Reliability, Authenticity, Simplicity, Completeness, Illustration, Location

WIIFM = What's In It For Me
            (It/This) will (Make/Give) you __results/emotion__

5 W's   =   Who, What, When, Where, Why

Now Let's Practice

WHO: _____

WHAT: _____

WHEN: _____

WHERE: _____

WHY: _____

More Practice: Putting It All Together

RASCIL >>>	**WHO**
RASCIL >>>	**WHAT**
	WHEN
	WHERE
	WHY <<< WIIFM

RASCIL = Reliability, Authenticity, Simplicity, Completeness, Illustration, Location

WIIFM = What's In It For Me
(It/This) will (Make/Give) you __results/emotion__

5 W's = Who, What, When, Where, Why

More Practice

WHO: _____

WHAT: _____

WHEN: _____

WHERE: _____

WHY: _____

Conclusion

This book provides a summary of how the media speaks to the public. The simple practice exercises allow for proficiency in any media event. In addition this book has created the foundation for guests to participate in a magazine article, 3 radio interviews and being profiled on TV on the web.

EPN provides this book to help guests do more for themselves and to create fantastic content. Even after EPN, this book is a valuable tool for future media events. That being said, the book has already paid for itself many times over.

Best wishes to your success !

www.ingramcontent.com/pod-product-compliance
Lightning Source LLC
Chambersburg PA
CBHW070838310526
45788CB00017B/2033